THE
GAME

JOHN OGDEN

Copyright © 2021 by John Ogden

All rights reserved.

No part of this publication may be reproduced, stored in a retrieval system or transmitted, in any form, or by any means, electronic, mechanical, recorded, photocopied, or otherwise, without the prior permission of the copyright owner, except by a reviewer who may quote brief passages in a review.

Printed in the United States of America

ISBN: 978-1-7351510-0-7

ACKNOWLEDGMENTS

Lets be honest, I wrote this book for me. I dragged myself onto a ledge on the mountain to access and review the climb from a better vantage point, hoping to map the way forward and challenge the peaks ahead.

I dedicate these words to my parents, Jill and Laurie Ogden, who gave the best start to life a boy could ever hope for.

I offer this story as an apology to my sisters—Sally, Wendy, Lyn, Lucy, and Clare—who I neglected and abandoned to go in search of the Philosopher's Stone.

For my brother, Kit, who pioneered many things, allowing me to follow steps behind—I owe you one.

To my wife for almost 40 years, Noriko, I recognize that she is the only one that can truly authenticate these life theories. Therefore, I request a stay of judgment, an extension of time, allowing me to practice the process!!

For the maestros mentioned within these pages, I offer my respect. Because of them, the doors and windows of my mind were opened. I could learn the rules of the game and start to play. I am grateful.

Aha, you have to read the book to discover who they are!!

To my daughter Kaori and her husband Dan, from the Naka family, who gave us the three munchkins—Emma, Ellie, and Louis—who hopefully are experiencing the "bubbling enthusiasm stage" mentioned in this book, I love you.

Last but not least, to the Big Kahuna, who built the deck and laid the cards on the table. We are coming to play, looking for another chance to win at this game.

> John Ogden
> July, 2020

FOREWORD

This book is written for me as I mentioned in the Acknowledgments. But just as Robert Mckee pointed out in the forward to *The War of Art*, it is written for you, too.

There will always be cries from the wilderness for a better understanding of the undeniable themes that run through the development of human history.

I lay claim to the possibility "that history has molded, moldy paradigms of thought that are so encrusted with barnacles that to uncover the truth is going to be virtually impossible." That statement, though harsh, is simply a call to arms.

Continuing in the same vein, I point out that "we have been duped to the fullest extent imaginable, not by malicious intent, though there are numerous players on that field, but by the cold hard rules of the game."

Therein lies the rub. What are these rules? Super intelligent men and women from all walks of life and persuasion have explored these avenues since time immemorial.

But, "let's be honest, deep down in our hearts something has not been explained very well." That's what this game is all about: explaining clearly the levels of love that we need to evolve through to mature. The origin of the difficulty—to establish irrefutable laws that have a common denominator relevant to all humanity—lies in this wondrous dynamic called "free will".

This book opens a conversation about that privilege. Even suggesting that the very diversity of Man stems from this source. Free will is a beautiful thing. Lets explore it together, adding our personal touches to the tapestry that history is weaving.

                              John Ogden
                              July, 2020

BOOK ONE

JOURNEY AND REFLECTIONS

by John Ogden

"Success is the progressive realization of a worthy goal or ideal"

—Earl Nightingale

but relax, it is also

"Success is stumbling from failure to failure with no loss of enthusiasm"

—Winston Churchill

2019, THE YEAR I FACED REALITY... AGAIN

It was quite a shock in the beginning because 2018 had stripped me bare. All the doors had been closed; the only place left was inside. And inside was not pretty.

When the fundamental belief structure that I had concocted for 35 years proved flawed and self-absorbed, it had taken years to establish a new game plan. The problem was this: the game was still deconstructing. I had begun 2019 wondering if I had hit bottom yet. All the pieces of the Life Puzzle were scattered across the floor, but there was a serious lack of conviction to put them back in better order.

WHEN REALITY HIT

For the last 7 years, I had read all the right books. Self-improvement begins with reading James Allen's, *As a Man Thinketh*, listening to Earl Nightingale's, *The Strangest Secret*, and throwing in a ton of Jim Rohn's material, starting with *The Challenge to Succeed* and *The Five Major Pieces of the Life Puzzle*. If you cannot hack the old-school stuff, at least go through them one time, then skip to Alexander Green's book of essays, *Beyond Wealth*, for a reminder of what is really important in life.

In addition to all the books I had read, I had received a mountain of very personal advice and consultation. Not surprisingly, I had narrowed down the origin of the problem to be squarely in the mirror in front of me.

But the real stunner came when I discovered that all the idealism and visionary hope for helping the world might as well have been pure poppycock because there was a prerequisite: to build a better model of myself first—or at least in conjunction with—saving the world. Ouch! When *that* reality hit, it really hurt.

You see, the progress behind the glass did not reflect that elusive ingredient called "result." The doors had shut because the secret lay behind only one door—the one door I needed to find for myself. Or at least I would have to pass through the only one left gaping wide before me.

What a way to begin a new year, waking up every day with a dull pain burrowing its way deeper and deeper into the emotional recesses of my heart.

LAYING THE FOUNDATIONS

I had learned some good fundamentals over the years. First, my British family upbringing taught me simple table manners, daily chores, a strong work ethic, and the value of family and friends. Later, in my 35-year odyssey into the religious world, I had added a few more. Freedom comes from "living right," "taking responsibility," and that elusive, all-important absolute: "getting a result."

Ahh, sounds simple enough, right? Good stuff to lay the foundations of a well-lived life. Oh, if we only knew!!! And what exactly is the "result" we are looking for? Therein lies the rub, yes, indeed. Getting clear on the nature of the result that insists on eluding us can entail a lifetime of tributary diversions. Streams meandering down centuries of time cannot answer that question explicitly. Why? Because we are endowed with an inalienable right from our Creator: a right called "free will."

FREE WILL

Free will. It's a beautiful thing; it's what makes us human. But it is also, possibly, the origin of the diversity. We all head off over the hill in different directions, with varying levels of will, determination, preparation, education, emotional fortitude, and planning. Couple that with pride, fear, and the clowns, ignorance, and arrogance, it's not surprising that we end up wandering somewhat aimlessly down memory lane, still trying to connect the dots.

If 'result' is everything (and I will climb out on my ledge and shout that it most certainly is!), then I ask again: What exactly is the result we are looking for?

Tough luck, kiddos. Did you think that would be a simple two-sentence answer? Not on your life! Pain and suffering are part and parcel of the Big Kahuna's design. Not because the Great Spirit has a mean streak, but simply because free will requires each of us to at least show a little sincerity and interest in "the game."

THE GAME

Ah-ha! It's *the game* we are talking about now. Achieving "results" is already up for debate—but *the game*? That requires participation, players, and teamwork. So where do we go from here?

News flash!!! Down the centuries of time, inspired individuals have led the way along the myriad of tributaries that I mentioned. They thought they had it all figured out. They raised their lamps and flooded the path ahead with their light. It might have been painstakingly difficult for them to make it to the river's edge; they sure as hell weren't going to stop and watch the river flow as Bob Dylan once exhorted us to do. Off they marched, grabbing "all and sundry" along the way.

I don't know for sure, but for every religious movement, there was probably some charismatic leader who first pioneered it. That's certainly true of every cult experiment, and possibly true of a whole lot of political persuasions as well. But wait! I am not inferring that that is bad, wrong, or inevitable. We need leaders, for sure. What I *am* suggesting is that we need to get in touch with *the result* and define the rules of *the game*.

TAKING RESPONSIBILITY

Back to January 2019. No doubt about it, I headed into this year with my tail between my legs. I had blown most of the inheritance my Dad left me on a wild and wonderful Crypto ride. Boy, did *that* come to a crushing halt in January of 2018!! By ignoring the basic rules of high-risk investment—to take out the profits as you go—I had lost my shirt.

After that, it was time to slink back to the hard grind of money for time. I am a very good driver—a professional one at that—except for the odd text. (Shhh!!! Don't tell anyone. Karma will catch up with me, as did the lesson on profit-taking.) As I had put that confession down on paper, I decided that texting should come to a screeching halt. All's well with my friend, Karma. No retroactive clauses implemented!!

So even as I set out to climb the hill of 2019 in low gear, the puzzle was still waiting at home each night; waiting for a piece to be added.

The moment came when I realized there was only one way to win at this game. I would have to take one deliberate step after another, starting very close to home—actually right inside. Step one? Take responsibility for cleaning my house and building a better relationship with my wife.

Ok, ok, how profound is that? Especially as the idea had come from my mentor, who cannot be named. He has a strict nondisclosure clause. Aha, careful now, no judgment or jumping to conclusions. Remember, we are looking to uncover "liquid gold," the "Holy Grail," what "real result" is, "in the big scheme of things."

To assist in those cleaning projects, I suggest the purchase of a unique book called, *The Life-Changing Magic of Tidying Up,* by Marie Kondo. It will turn into a therapeutic, almost spiritual experience!!!

So the result was left out to dry for a while, even though I had hinted pretty strongly where the rubber met the road. The game needs to be played well, because progress in the result category, will only come about if we are rolling the dice. Rolling the dice in the game of life requires a heavy dose of sincerity, more than a smattering of desire to know what is authentic and what is real. Truckloads of trucks to take away the failed attempts, and probably a boatload of time.

MY EPIPHANY

At the beginning of January, I had experienced an epiphany of sorts. The desire was there to at least mold some kind of wisdom into my collective failures. The idea morphed into a pretty attractive excuse that would allow me to survive another year or two, at least. It went something like this: the reality is the learning curve is "paced" differently for everyone. Those of us destined to walk the long way home have the wonderful job of concocting all manner of excuses along the way. Believe me we have to, just to be able to keep motating, that is, eh, growing and staying alive.

What I had concluded was that there is a correlation among the accumulated failed attempts, time, effort, emerging wisdom, and forgiveness from the Divine. At some point, He throws up his arms and says, "I better give the guy a break this year, or he ain't going to make it over the next hump."

There is nothing better than a flush of positivity flowing through one's veins that counter to public opinion and most everyone's conclusions: this guy has finally tipped the scale!!!

An element of progress has been made by default; accumulated failures eventually mature into "radiant sunshine." Yeah baby, I believe. I paid the piper and I am free to collect my winnings.

I know, I know, poppycock again you say, "result" will only come from a specific plan, first drafted in your mind, then transferred to pen and paper, and finally, implemented with discipline and fortitude.

That's all true, but for many of us we are not endowed with the attributes of the likes of Napoleon Hill of *Think and Grow Rich* fame. But guess what? That last sentence is not strictly true "*if* we are still in the game."

THE TWO P'S

2019 is my living proof that persistence pays off. Read Napoleon Hill's, *Outwitting the Devil*, published around 2011, but written in 1939, if I remember correctly. Yes, hidden for more than seventy years. It tells the real story of Napoleon Hill's blood, sweat, and tears to make it into the "sunshine." He suffered adversities and setbacks that seeded the inspiring message of *Think and Grow Rich*. How did he manage that? And as a side note, I don't care that an article recently emerged questioning the veracity of various facts and Napoleon Hill's account of encounters with famous figures that he wove into his *Think and Grow Rich* story. What counts, is that he epitomized the basic prerequisite required.

Persistence and Perseverance: Dance Until It Rains, is the title of a book waiting to be read sitting on my desk. Instinct had told me that those two p's are required when all else has come to a grinding halt. What do the Marines say? "Failure is not an option." Therefore, we need to P, P, and carry on.

Of course, persistence and perseverance are just the tools to keep the wolves at bay while the rules of the game are revisited and clarified, results assessed, and a more focused plan formulated. In other words, we have to evaluate the mountain of failures for what they are: uh, duh, *failures* or *things that did not work*. Hopefully, because we have a good accumulation of them under our belt, we can consciously turn towards the North Face of the Eiger (the mountain we should have been climbing) and settle into basecamp, ready to move our sorry arses in a more productive direction.

THE GAME OF LIFE

Time for a paradigm shift. The game is simple in name, but a thousand times more difficult and complicated than we had been led to believe. The game of life is the evolution of our ability to love and grow (spiritually). The difficulty is that love is not one big basket of hippiedom fame ("Make love and peace, man…"). It is the quiet evolution of stages of development that hopefully we have experienced, as we moved through life from an infant to a grandparent, and beyond: into community.

SETTING THE STAGE

At this point, I will be entering into some level of plagiarism. This information is the intellectual property of my aforementioned mentor. He is in the process of writing his first book on the topic, due out in 2021.

So while we wait with bated breath for the authentic version, I will set the stage and lay some groundwork. I will prepare you in fact, for the disillusionment to follow.

Yes, news flash two, we have been duped to the fullest extent imaginable. Mostly not by malicious intent—though, of course, there are numerous players on that field—but by the cold, hard rules of the game.

There is "no compromise," and as I mentioned once before, we are here to "grow" in our ability to "love." Also, because it's worth a second reminder, "free will" is the culprit for the long and winding road. Yes sir, yes ma'am, start digesting those little observations and their historical ramifications.

This might be a good moment to issue a couple of disclaimers and the odd FYI. As you might have deduced, this man is not the smartest tool in the shed, and he willingly attests to zero claims to fame or to fortune. The notches on my belt are carved by time and circumstance. The vision is derived by personal experience, large family upbringing, world travel, numerous jobs from a young age including farming, construction, steel fixing, woodworking, and business ownership in Auto Transport. As well as various religious forays beginning with Quakerism, one ongoing arranged marriage in the Unification Church to an oriental girl, which brought one child only, not by choice, but the desire for a large family curtailed by medical difficulty. There is further character tempering being administered as we speak, by three grandchildren and of course, lest we forget, the myriad aforementioned failures that can seriously rock one's boat.

Yes, yes, yes, duly noted, serious lack of formal education, college dropout to boot, are partially the origin of the problem we might be encountering here. Ah, ah, careful now, five years of world travel and a lifetime enrollment in the University of Hard Knocks put me in a category of experience that most university students could not even imagine, let alone have accomplished.

Touché!! Yes, yes, yes, of course, we are dealing with damaged goods. Lack of self-esteem and a lifetime without confidence or focus, various other maladies to boot, are part and parcel of the package sitting on the step of my life.

Gullibility has duly reared its head for huge spans of the journey, but the quiet optimist remains. Indefatigable, pulsating, wounded, sheepishly glancing around, thinking, how the f*** did this all happen to me without me really noticing? Excuse my French, but really, we surely deserve a better education system in "The Life" category than "progress by default."

So now you have a small insight into at least one player on the field, but before we return to the mountain and base camp, let's clarify a few more facts and figures.

This boy has opened a Pandora's box of discussion topics. He has thrown a few barbs at the religious world already: they will need to be clarified, and he will be held accountable. But 35 years—actually 40 come April 4th this year—is foundational work that allows freedom of speech. The last five or more, he has spent time dabbling in the self-improvement world, and in the next few pages, barbs will fly in that direction as well. He is not looking for, or even expecting much, from any camp. Rules of engagement need to be set, that's all. The game needs to be clarified and introduced to a wider audience. So that is the basic purpose of this book.

MY PURPOSE

Here is a little observation in that context, penned by yours truly a few years back:

"My passion is simple. I believe we could solve all kinds of problems from the individual, through the family, to the national level, by simply better dialog. Now to move towards that dream (haha), we will need a more universal terminology than religion, and many cults, creeds, and even philosophies have come up with."

Sounds a bit idealistic, and it is, but it is amazing how communication can improve if people get down and dirty and have a real dialogue about their strong opinions. The catch is, they have to follow rules of respect and such like. The *real* catch is that they have to stay in the game to have any chance to come up with any semblance of collective wisdom. Most people get indignant and head for the security of their own blanket.

If you can relate to any of that, it would be a start, but the reality is not pretty. From suicide, to murder, to war, we have examples of humanity's inability to sit down and "have a cuppa" (You have to be British to know what that means…. It begins with 'T' if you need a hint.)

So better dialogue requires better language. Six thousand years of recorded history has not managed to cut the mustard, in my humble opinion. I like the approach of one Stephen Pressfield in his groundbreaking book, *The War of Art*. Not to be confused with *The Art of War*, though Pressfield is a worthy Shogun in my book. In *The War of Art*, he maps out what it takes to do the work of being a writer. In expletives that warm the working man's soul, he lays the responsibility for everything back at the feet of the writer/reader. In terminology that has potential universal recognition, he introduces the bad guy. Remember him? The Rolling Stones wrote a symphony in his honor, big D, yes, yes, yes, well Pressfield quietly calls him Resistance. Mmm… I like that. The whole book steers clear of religious waffle, which I also like because religious terminology has befuddled the minds of vast swaths of humanity down through time immemorial. Yet again, what I also like is this: in the last chapter, he hints at the origin of his creativity as coming from Muses and Angels.

Anyway, enough said, read the book. I don't agree with all his conclusions, and you might not either, but the work, the work, is anvil strong and door-opening material.

REFLECTIONS

So disclaimer time again… FYI, or whatever you want to call it. It must seem like I am talking with "forked tongue." Do I believe? Do I not believe? Patience my friends, this is ocean deep stuff. History has molded moldy paradigms of thought that are so encrusted with barnacles that to uncover the truth is going to be virtually impossible.

Perhaps this is a good moment for the exodus from my book of all those arrogant enough to believe that the material world, and the world of emotion and will is all that exists in this vast universe of things.

I will take this opportunity to shoot my first barb in the direction of the self-improvement world. That world is super smart, but almost to a man, they do not mess with the mess of the religious world; talk about Pandora's boxes. I know, not a hope in hell of any consensus coming out of that conversation, so they steer clear. I can respect that, but how are we going to chart the territory then? Because a map without spiritual coordinates will never ever take us into the sunshine.

Yes, I have to go out on my ledge again and pay homage to the center of the universe. We can call it what we like, but it is there—Divinity, Spirit—pulsating, indefatigable, unchanging… it cannot even be damaged. It is made of Kryptonite; it is what bonds love into being. That's as far as I will go on that topic right now. I don't know enough about that arena yet, but I know it's there, and if you're honest, so do you. Let's just call it Divinity because we will need some kind of terminology when we go back to base camp and start climbing the mountainside.

To be fair, I have to recognize at least one wayfarer from the self-improvement world that has no fear of the word or world of "Spirit." That would be Mr. Bob Proctor. He recognizes the cornerstone of the Universe and teaches powerfully about how to awaken the sleeping giant that we are, by bridging the gap to that inner world. "If you build it, they will come."

As I have yet to really step into the arena of plagiarism, maybe now is a good time to throw out a baited hook from halfway up the mountainside—just to keep you awake and curious. Even only halfway up is rarefied air, uncharted territory, unprecedented, with few examples available. That camp is called Spiritual Adolescence; it is where the rubber meets the road. Here we have to finally take responsibility and find out things for ourselves. Make mistakes and pay the price. Hopefully, there is parental support, at least, and ideally, community-level assistance, but good luck with that. This level of maturity should, as all the others, be age-related. Late teens would be nice, but good luck with that, too!! Here, the young man or woman has walked away from all the suggestions and solutions offered by all and sundry. They have consciously turned inward, seeking enlightenment from the soul, from Divinity, and through "engagement" with that Divinity. They have actually experienced and tasted a level of love to build their life upon. The connection has been made; I am who I am. I know the source of existence, and I will work from here to climb higher and higher. I will look for a fellow climber and choose to rope the two of us together, to challenge the peaks ahead in conjugal love, parental love, and more.

That's a taste; we can't afford to underestimate the difficulties at this level. We need to be searching with heart and soul, uncovering the source of everything and approaching enlightenment, becoming a man or a woman.

Maybe we can get there together, but I doubt it. Just as those who can't envision the world of Spirit, left a few pages ago, so all of you will be gone sooner or later. For the most part, people are just curious, happy to be fed information. When it comes down to work in spiritual mountaineering, they disappear back to the security of their own blanket. We are survivalists; the job is bringing home the bacon, the weekend is fast approaching. We are good people… isn't that enough? Nope. Remember, no compromise.

Let's head to base camp. Don't get too excited; most people never leave the valley, so it's not going to be too crowded. We will recognize those, like ourselves, wondering how the heck we ended up against the cliff. The starry-eyed enthusiasts, all smiles, will greet us expecting to head out at first light. Let's see how long it takes to burst their bubbles. There will be a host of lookers. When the going gets tough, they will slip away one by one to lick their wounds, back in the valley of friends. Nothing wrong with that. At least they made it into the clearinghouse. Let's be fair, quite a cross-section of humanity makes it to the mountainside; man is surprisingly resilient when it comes to exploring the game of life.

As we look around, if we are lucky, we will catch sight of a few professionals: steely-eyed, weathered, calm, back from the climb. Nobody is ever going to pull the wool over their eyes again. They have tasted the rarefied air, sweet as nectar. But as setbacks occur, reboots are needed.

If we are smart, we will seek their council, sleep near their tent. But don't think for a minute that they came back to help. Helping others as a means of fulfillment is the love of brothers and sisters; they have experienced that already. It is only three steps removed from the love that an infant needs. The territory they have just explored is a paradigm shift away. Rarefied air, remember; unprecedented. Come down from there and look around carefully. It's very easy to be pessimistic. Humanity is still in the dark ages spiritually. Most people don't even have a clue that they are meant to be climbers, how much less are they conscious of the steps required.

Ok, ok, that's a little cold, but no compromise is absolute. They say, "All the words have been said already, there is no new truth." But look at the messed up lives of the masters that produced the classics in music and verse. Love is a many-splendored thing, for sure, but even though they said all the words in beautiful prose, let's be honest—deep down in our hearts, something has not been explained very well.

That's what this game is all about, explaining clearly the levels of love that we need to evolve through to mature. We also need to clarify the rules of engagement involved as we enter that engagement with the Divine, as we are tested, climbing the ropes of maturity.

Disclaimer time again. (I better stop trying to number them. This book will be so full of excuses you might end up wondering what the heck this boy is talking about—if you don't already!!) The analogy to mountaineering has to be taken with a pinch of salt. The first three camps will hopefully not be experienced on the mountainside!! Our kids are thrown to the wolves as it is, without us really understanding the sponge effect the young mind is capable of. Throwing them out in the snow as well would be considered abandonment, for sure.

Anyway… continuing on, regardless!!

Camp One is the infant stage level of love. It's a one-way street, gimme gimme gimme, feed me, clean me, hug me, shelter me from harm. Then do it again, and again, and again… I might smile after six months—if you're lucky.

It's foundational work. Trust and love are building blocks of the best life ever. Imagine the consequences of any deficiency at this time. Instead of a kaleidoscope of joy in a bubbling, blossoming heart, seeds of fear and neglect are planted. Puzzlement creeps in with inhibition in tow, and the long and winding road sets off in the wrong direction. Ok, ok, little melodramatic, but you get my drift?

BOOK TWO

LEVELS OF LOVE

by John's mentor

> Sections from John's mentor will appear like this, with text in a tinted box.

*Love can only be experienced in
relationship with "other."*

*Love is an experience of the "self."
Its perspective is from the "I."*

*The degree of maturation of love
at each level: 0% to 100%.*

*There is a point where one attains
the "essence" of that level.*

Camp 1 "The Infant Stage"

The Feeling of Self

The infant stage is the base level of love, the unconditional love. It is the feeling of "being loved," "being wanted." It is also the feeling of "feeling secure."

The Characteristic of the Other

A completely embracing energy, always there for you 24/7 (a motherly trait), and non-judgmental. Also seen as the Provider and Protector (a "fatherly" trait).

When you improperly experience this level, you constantly seek love by:

 a. trying to receive it directly from someone else

 b. taking the role of the Giver of that love (by giving it, you are trying to give it to yourself)

When you get stuck at this level, you overemphasize the need for unconditional love. (That is all you need.)

REFLECTIONS CONT...

So disclaimer time again… FYI, or whatever you want to call it. A few pages back, where I asked, "You get my drift?" I began my first full-on plagiaristic statement. It doesn't quite feel right, but so be it, no turning back, the cat is out of the bag, the genie fled the lamp. We need this. Continuing in plagiaristic mode…

Camp 2 "Early Childhood"

The Feeling of Self

This is the energy of feeling accepted and approved, acknowledged by the other.

The Characteristic of the Other

Engaged in love, seeing the individual making decisions and choices. Guiding them with love, supporting their choices, interjecting only when danger is in sight. Often seen as "Parent," "Teacher," "Master," "Lord." When you improperly experience this level, you constantly seek the love by being involved in relationships that make you feel accepted, acknowledged, or being the one "ideal" authority figure for others. When you get stuck at this level, there is an overemphasis on rules and hierarchy; doing what is right to please the authority figure, being obedient, focused on purity, or the reward/punishment paradigm.

Camp 3 "Later Childhood"

The Feeling of Self

Feeling of "brotherhood"/ "sisterhood," "camaraderie." A feeling of cohesion, togetherness, unison. "One for All, All for One." A feeling of being accepted/loved within a group.

The Characteristic of the Other

Care and compassion towards others; feels the suffering of others. Such feelings can often lead to fighting against injustice, a concept of "living for the sake of others," "To sacrifice for the whole." Heroes and Saviors. John Lennon's song, "Imagine."

When "overdone" at this level, the Self is lost in the Whole. The goal is towards Peace... to end suffering, the dryness/emptiness of being the hero.

REFLECTIONS CONT...

So we will need to go to the mountainside to get any vision of the next level of love.

Camp 4 "Adolescent Stage"

The Feeling of Self

Feeling of "Self-fulness" vs. "Selfishness" The liberating feeling of discovering and knowing who you really are. A fullness feeling that is springing forth from within."

The Characteristic of the Other

"Holding a space," being there with minimal interference, anticipatory excitement of the "blossoming." Such feelings can often lead to confident, charismatic, magnetic, independent, courageous, "sure of one's self," "I am the Christ," "I am enlightened,' When overdone at this level, a false sense of wholeness and completion, arrogance, dictatorial, infallible, non-team player.

REFLECTIONS CONT...

Let's get back to earth, no more camps. The mountainside is for the adolescent experience.

Camp 5: Conjugal Love

Characteristics

From One to Two, Image of the Dance. The two never become one. The two dance together around each other. To intimately share with another. Fullness by oneself (adolescence). Greater fullness with the other (conjugal). Misconceptions: Chemistry: Dysfunction meeting Dysfunction.

- **Infant stage:** Spouse is Provider/Unconditional love.

- **Early Childhood Stage:** Spouse is the one who approves/accepts.

- **Later Childhood Stage:** Spouse is the one who serves and sacrifices.

- **Adolescent Stage:** Spouse is the Charismatic, confident being.

REFLECTIONS CONT...

We get married, with each person bringing disparate levels of love to the table.

Camp 6: Parental Stage

From 2 to 3, to be able and allowed to participate in the growth of the individual (levels 1-6). In delight to see an individual blossoming into maturity.

Misconceptions

Parental love emphasis at different stages.

- **Infant Stage:** Parent teaches you to have unconditional love.
- **Early Childhood Stage:** Parent teaches you to obey.
- **Later Childhood Stage:** Parent wants you to be selfless.
- **Adolescent Stage:** Parent wants you to do what makes you happy.
- **Conjugal Stage:** Marry and enjoy being together.

Camp 7: Communal

One cell vs. One body. Mature families coming together to build communities that support the levels of growth of love.

Camp 8: Grandparental

Experience at a distance, no responsibilities, just "pure enjoyment."

FREE WILL, BABY, IT'S A BEAUTIFUL THING

Well that was several pages of undiluted plagiarism, which you have received without the classroom experience from the authentic creator. Oh well, so be it.

The exit from my book, I have already predicted, so go where you may.

For those that the bell rings, or tingles at least, a waking soul, just read those pages again with a paradigm shift mind. I will go out on my ledge and shout, "This is potential human evolution material from the spiritual dark ages to the cradle of humanity's desire to love."

Why hasn't it been explained well before? Bloody good question. Been asking myself the same thing for the last seven years, but as I said already, "It's a thousand times more difficult than we were led to believe and the pomp and circumstance and barnacles that have encrusted the thought of man, down narrow tunnels of delusion, never cease to amaze. Free will, baby, it's a beautiful thing."

The Divinity that we are trying to elicit relationship with doesn't even engage with the base level existence that is continually being flaunted. She doesn't force, she doesn't coerce, she doesn't cajole. She will walk away for 400 years if necessary, while we collapse into that "dark age" or another of our making.

So you're still not feeling me?

No worries mates, as the Aussies say, come back in three years, or thirty, after you have swung for the hills on your own mountainside. If the hickory you're using doesn't sing with a slap of love, eventually, you will have to turn back time and come to the North Face. There will be consolation prizes; you will be older and wiser. Like Edison, you will have eliminated ways that did not light your lamp. Like Edison, you might have secured your material future, so the pain will have dulled away anyway!!

THE LEVELS OF LOVE

Let's be fair; be proud of whatever you accomplish. Fantastic people operate at all the levels of love, they plant their flag and the Universe responds. There are many ways to skin a cat.

My passion is simple: explain this game and build a team of players who are willing to explore the North Face just in case humanity has missed some hidden jewels; just in case the very purpose of life has been neglected because we did not know the step by step process of growing our ability to love.

THE MASTERS OF LIFE

Disclaimer time again, I have already made some inaccurate observations. For instance, there are numerous players in the self-improvement arena that lay claim to being masters at education in the "life category"—and they are!! Three of the very best I have already mentioned: Jim Rohn, Bob Proctor, and Napoleon Hill. I could suggest ten more, beginning with John Maxwell, Darren Hardy, Les Brown, Tony Robbins, and a slew more!!!! Hats off to each of them. They opened my eyes to add context to the "religious world."

Oh yeah, just in case you think I am avoiding the masters from that world and their monumental achievements—relax. Remember, this boy has 40 years in that game. From Jesus to Mohammed, to the modern-day prophets, such as Reverend Sun Myung Moon, who I worked with for 35 years. These people are powerful, charismatic juggernauts, and they turn the direction of history. It will take another book to explain the consequences of their actions, and even though I previously promised to elaborate, let's stay on track in the search for the result and the game.

THE "PROCESS"

Have the pages of plagiarism caused confusion or planted a seed? Hopefully, the latter. Obviously, there is a need for a lifetime of elaboration!! Here's hoping you're all a quick study—sharper tools in the shed than yours truly—because I am going to jump to the "process," the method to evolve and regulate progress in the "game."

That's where we will head for now. Buckle up or run for the hills. My favorite line is always appropriate!!! Free will, baby, it's a beautiful thing.

DIVINITY

If you had read Pressfield's, *The War of Art*, you would have experienced his disdain for the words "support" or "workshop." He is adamant that the buck stops right at home in the center of the mirror. His forceful assertion of that requirement is profound and crucial to "spiritual adolescence," but let's face it, life can be lonely and hard as it is. So as Pressfield elicits reluctant admission of Muses and Angels, so too in *The Game*, I am going to entertain continual reference to Divinity. Luckily for us, Divinity is one step up from Muses and Angels, so we are in good company!!!

Why not God instead of Divinity you might well ask, and that would be a good question. My simple answer goes like this:

If you have had your name taken in vain, proselytized, stomped on, used in the manipulation of vast swaths of humanity down through time immemorial, you might have been open to a couple of aliases to try on for size. Relax—we already decided to call it any which way you like. Divinity evokes a softer touch.

THE RULES OF THE GAME

So all that waffle was just the intro to the rules of the game. This is a team sport, baby. The rules are simple, straightforward, and practical. Oh, did I say they were easy? Nope. As I said, a thousand times more difficult than we were led to believe. If they were easy, some other dreamer would have mapped them out already (and they might have made the required reading list in high school, or at least subbed for Animal Farm or such like). Good luck with that. Even the great self-improvement educator, Stephen Covey (or rather, his son, because Stephen passed away at 75 along with Wayne Dyer and Jim Rohn—who all passed at 75). Stephen's son has struggled to get *The Seven Habits of Highly Effective People* into the education system. That's ten times smarter guys than me, laying it all out on the line.

Interesting!!!! What is wrong with us? Supposedly all the words have been said already. There is no new truth, yet we wallow in the spiritual Dark Ages like we did not have a clue. Free will baby, it's a beautiful thing.

The rules of the game go like this...

RULE #1

First and foremost, an attitude of sincerity is required, coupled with an open-minded willingness to entertain the possibility that a lot of what you have been taught needs to be questioned. As I said, powerful narrow tunnels of delusion have been propagated down through history. These thought patterns have been molded by religious connotations and other charismatic leaders' conclusions. Up on their high horses, they raised their flags and charged down through history, winging it as they went. They molded the populaces to their beck and call because the appearance of something better enticed many onto the playing field. Fortunately, many times it was better and history progressed.

Excuse my cynicism, but do you get my drift?

Here is where the rest of you—those who cannot stomach spiritual inference—will head for the hills. Please read *The War of Art* on the way out. As I already said, Muses and Angels were Pressfield's reluctant admission; mine is Divinity.

RULE #2

Rule Number Two is a continuation of the first. Along with sincerity, we have to be good students, good listeners, and active participants.

RULE #3

Rule Number Three is explicit. If you are sincere and engage in the game, knock and the door will be opened; seek and you will find. Sadly, very religious connotations, but they will elicit a response from Divinity. Just as there is no compromise, Divinity is bound by irrefutable laws of love to reciprocate. Just remember you are here to grow, so the manner of response might not necessarily be to your liking. Actually, heart-rending tendencies will come up that will require our reluctant admission. Oh yeah, I knew I had to work on that relationship or another!!

Many of the responses will go right over your head, others might kick you in the nuts; so be careful of what you ask for. More than occasionally, tender grace will descend to keep your head above water. The color of gratitude better seep through your canvas on those days. This is a working climb remember, so get up quick when you go down. Remember, we already decided this was not going to be easy and we agreed to be sincere.

THE RESULT

Little by little, the response pattern will emerge. Hey, there is something to this game; the Universe responds, Spirit is real. Answers are uncovered, eyes are opened, authentic, personal experiences are had that make the pain worthwhile. OMG, is my heart getting bigger? Good luck with that, watch out for the slap in the face as arrogance tries to creep in.

A JUDGMENT-FREE ZONE

Disclaimer time again, now you must be considering that I finally just tricked you into another religious nomenclature. This all sounds like regurgitated faith requirements. Of course, it is in a way. Remember, mostly there is no new truth; all the words have been said already. But the Divinity we are trying to elicit relationship with wears different clothes to the color that has been drummed into our hearts for 2,000 years as a Christian, or 4,000 as a Jew. Just as there is no compromise, Divinity has no judgment. Period. Did you hear that clearly?

> The Divine NEVER judges when you are falling down making mistakes. He is there to support you in love, encouraging you to grow up.

That's my first plagiaristic sentence for a while. Read it again, and think about it clearly. It's quite logical, really—simply a true parental level of love.

Maybe it's time for a plagiaristic page that summarizes The Rules of the Game. It's a simplified page, but balances my waffle quite nicely.

Rules of Engagement

1. Sincerity of Desire. True sincerity comes with courage and action.

2. Being a "Good Student." Being a good listener and active participant.

3. If you engage, there will be a response. Be careful what you ask for!!!

4. The response to your question is always "right." 95% homework, 5% grace.

5. Over time, we need to develop our Spiritual Senses. This will help us to have greater intuitive discernment.

6. Continual Effort: Don't worry about failing. Just get up and do it again with sincerity. Never judge yourself.

"You" are the driver, not the Divine.
("Humans have Free Will")

The Divine NEVER judges when you are falling down, making mistakes. He is there to support you in Love, encouraging you to grow up.

The Divine engages most with those who are "Good Students," those who are willing to reach higher and higher levels of Love.

The Rules of Engagement applies to both worlds:

1. Living in this world: Developing your talents and abilities.
2. Internal world: Development of Internal Character and Capacities of Love

THE ROAD OF RESPONSIBILITY

So there you go, from the horse's mouth. Now you're probably thinking, what's so difficult about all that, it's just a twist on an old recipe. I will give it a go and give you a report next week.

Go ahead, light a fire, raise a flag. As I have inferred, you're all probably smarter tools in the shed than me, so hopefully, giant steps will be made in the first weeks and months. Good luck with that!!

But when time slips away, life's distractions take over and blanks are drawn. Just go back over some of the observations mentioned. Whether it is, "We are survivalists, the job is bringing home the bacon," "We are good people—isn't that enough?" or, "She doesn't force, she doesn't coerce, she doesn't cajole, she will walk away for 400 years if necessary, while we collapse into that dark age or another of our making."

The real kicker is this (and I have said it 10 times already): Free will, it's a beautiful thing.

We are endowed with inalienable rights from our Creator, as you have heard, from higher sources than me. The one that needs to be elucidated once in a while, is that of "Co-Creatorship." The Big Kahuna covered all the bases except that one minor detail: we are responsible for creating ourselves, our spirit, our love, our being. There is no compromise. Are we willing to walk down that road of responsibility?

Like I said already, most people do not have a clue that they're meant to be climbers, let alone be aware of the steps required.

Technically, we should be jumping for joy. Despite all that appears to be manipulating us, pulling us in this direction or another, we are actually "free" people. We are in the driver's seat. 100 percent responsible for creating our spirit and our ability to love. Not a bad deal at all, considering all the stuff we get for free.

Of course, "the cascade of confusion history" might not have left us with the realization that growing our ability to love was the most important thing in the Universe to work on.

THE ABILITY TO LOVE

News flash #3: it's a paradigm shift to even approach that understanding. As if you hadn't noticed, love is subtle and shy, elusive, and quiet. She doesn't shout from the mountain tops and she won't put up being trampled on or betrayed. Let's be honest though—undermining everything, subtly portrayed everywhere, pumping like blood from the heart—she is calling to be heard.

Of course, society's portrayal of love is slightly distorted at best and totally screwed up at worst. Hello!! The point being, oh yeah, she is out there calling, everywhere, all the time. At least admit that much. Do you get my drift? Much of pop music, country music, and more, are playing that tune.

I digress a little to be quite honest. We are meant to be exploring the mountainside; learning how to engage with the Divine as we climb the ropes of maturity, how to grow spiritually, how to check ourselves, and most importantly, how to fill the gaps in our gaping lack of experience of the different levels of love as we grew up. Yeah, yeah, yeah, you guys had all the love you ever needed in all the right proportions, and all at the right time to boot. Be patient with the rest of us.

THE PLAYING FIELD

As I said repeatedly, it's a paradigm shift to even approach these concepts and to realize that they are paramount. It will probably take my mentor's book, which isn't even written, plus his content and wisdom, to even entice you onto the playing field.

Here is the paradox. You think it might be hard enticing you guys onto the playing field? Well, I have news for you ladies and gentlemen, I will need some serious help to get him to even take a second look.

Remember I said, "On the mountainside, we might bump into a few professionals, steely-eyed, calm? Nobody is ever going to pull the wool over their eyes again?" But I also said, "Don't think for a minute that they came back to help; they have experienced that already." Helping others is the love of brothers and sisters. It's only two steps removed from the love that an infant needs.

Stephen Pressfield is 100% right. The buck stops right there in the center of the mirror.

Here I am dreaming of "support" and "workshops," the very epitome of what does not work in adolescence, when we haven't even got a team of "players" to start the game (let alone those well trained and serious enough to coach others)!

Interesting… I've probably lost the rest of you completely now. Lol.

The main man is only willing to teach this stuff to sincere students who are ready to get down and dirty and have a real dialogue about the process. He is tired and frighteningly aware that it is almost a lost cause to even attempt to turn the tide of history.

What did I say awhile back? It's a thousand times more difficult than we were led to believe; and the pomp and circumstance and barnacles that have encrusted the thought of man, down narrow tunnels of delusion, never cease to amaze.

The best that most charismatic leaders bring to the table, even the good ones, is a slight variation on an existing theme. How many Christian denominations are there? Right!!! Say no more. At least the Jews have been consistent in their stubbornness. Just a few variations on a basic story.

Relax, all you religious types that have hung in there patiently waiting for the full biblical explanation and confirmation of these theories… It ain't coming! Sorry to burst your bubbles. Just like the starry-eyed enthusiasts who operate, fluctuating between level 2 and level 3 on the "Love Barometer," you guys are going to have to dig deep to even comprehend what level you are operating on. I will let you down easy by not even suggesting the paradigm that you are working in. Start the journey. It will take a while. Remember, I have 40 years in that game. So those of you who are beginning to lose your cool because it sounds like you're not going to get what you expected in the time frame you're used to—relax, patience is a virtue. Catch it if you can. I sound British, again.

THE TEST OF TIME

There's another kicker: time frame. We have to rethink everything we have learned. Because of "Free Will," the road has been long and wide and continually set off in sometimes catastrophic directions. Communism for example, Hitlerism, White Supremacy, to name but a few. We have to really dig deep to get our minds around the consequences of free will. Holy Moses, has it been worth the price?

Oh, yeah! Absolutely! We would not have it any other way. What a tapestry we have managed to paint. From societal majesty at times, can't think of any right now, lol, though I was awfully tempted to say British. Jeeze, I am in trouble. I sat for a good five minutes trying to come up with a true societal majesty, but my mind is blank. American comes second to mind because the Founding Fathers rolled out some pretty impressive rules of the game. But then we have to admit, the baggage attached and the bloodshed that ensued—nah, not so impressive. There is a little island off the coast of India or Africa, forgot its name right now, that's taking a pretty impressive shot at multi-cultural living.

Let's not even go down the other extreme, from the Holocaust to Rwanda. Too diabolical to contemplate.

Hey, I think I just made a pretty good case for the need for this book.

"Mature families coming together to build communities that support the levels of growth of love." Dream on, baby.

ON A FINAL NOTE

Well, it's almost time. Let's draw this "story" to a close. We have plenty of work to do while we wait with bated breath for the authentic version. 2020 is slipping away, so with a little help from all my newfound friends out there, let's see what we can prepare.

> "He is not looking for, or even expecting much, from any camp. Rules of Engagement need to be set, that's all. The game needs to be clarified and introduced to a wider audience. So that is the basic purpose of this book."

Those are my words, by the way.

For those for whom this content "wakes a sleeping soul," and for the "steely-eyed professionals" who know exactly what I am talking about, my question is this: Are we team players? Are we willing to come to base camp with humble hearts? Both are serious questions because together, when we knock on the doctor's door and he agrees to a round table, we will have to dig deep to understand the profound underlying dynamic that he lives by. (He is a Naturopathic doctor in real life, by the way. Don't hold that against him.) It is to do with free will and the requirements of the Rules of Engagement.

Come to explore; it's a team sport, baby. Let's play!

To be notified for my mentor's book when it is completed, sign up on the waitlist below, as well as for any upcoming news that I will be sending out.

www.levelsoflove101.com

John Ogden
July 2020

www.ingramcontent.com/pod-product-compliance
Lightning Source LLC
Chambersburg PA
CBHW071029080526
44587CB00015B/2549